Table of Contents

Introduction 2
Fabric Requirements 3

Month One
Hexagon Blocks 4
Hummingbird Blocks 6
Flourishing Leaf Blocks 8

Month Two
Bowties Blocks 12

Month Three
Garden of Eden Blocks 14

Month Four
Puzzle Star Blocks 16

Month Five
Mosaic Blocks 18

Month Six
Big Block One 20

Month Seven
Big Block Two 22

Month Eight
Quilt Center & Inner Border 26

Month Nine
Queen Outer Border & Finishing 30
King Outer Border & Finishing 32

Introduction

About the Quilt

There is no other art quite like quilting that connects us to our past and the quilters who came before us. No matter what difficulties, challenges and troubles the era brought, quilters persisted in finding and making beautiful things. Through the years, the Aunt Grace fabric collections from Marcus Fabrics have reliably become It's Sew Emma's favorite window to the early twentieth century. Fabric designer Judie Rothermel has yet again gone through her treasure trove of collected scraps to assemble something new from something old, fittingly named Aunt Grace Baskets of Scraps.

With these charming 1930s feedsack prints, we have cultivated a quilt in the same fashion, combining the old and new into something lovely and refreshing. All of the blocks in this book are familiar, tried-and-true classics, but they have been finished with original elements and techniques that we know you will enjoy! The patchwork border was selected as the perfect illustration of how our smallest pieces, our "basket of scraps", can combine to form one of our favorite elements of this quilt.

Helpful Tidbits & Notions

The same fabric requirements for the quilt top can be used to make either the queen or king versions of this quilt. From each colored print used in this quilt, you will save strips to subcut later for the outer border. Flip to page 30 and page 32 and you will see how the same number of strips can yield the amount of patchwork squares you will need for either the queen or king borders.

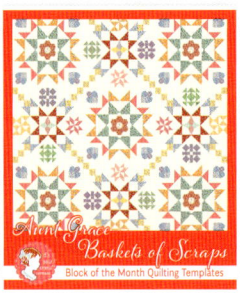

For the appliqué blocks in this quilt, you may be glad to know there is not a stitch of paper piecing used at all! The appliqué is designed to mimic the look of paper piecing without the extra work. In addition, we have included templates at actual size in the book, but we have also made a set of Aunt Grace Baskets of Scraps Impressions Templates you can use instead. The four plastic templates are full-scale and printed with helpful lines and placement guides. We prefer to use these templates since it saves the time needed to prepare the appliqué pieces, and it is a goof-proof method for us!

To match the vibrant colors in this quilt, we have also curated a beautiful box of fine, strong Aurifil 50 weight cotton thread. It contains 10 spools selected to blend right into your fabric.

You can purchase these notions at www.ItsSewEmma.com.

Basic Piecing and Applique Instructions

We do not recommend pre-washing your fabric. Use a ¼" seam, 2.0 stitch length and follow the pressing arrows shown in the diagrams. We made our quilt using the needle-turn method of applique, but you can use your favorite method. All templates are printed at actual size and do not include seam allowances. Most importantly, enjoy making this quilt!

Fabric Requirements

Month One

	5901-2174	2 ¾ yards
	8080-311	½ yard
	8083-311	⅜ yard
	8086-335	⅜ yard
	8079-326	⅜ yard
	8080-333	⅜ yard
	8082-314	⅜ yard
	8084-322	½ yard
	8082-335	½ yard
	8085-322	⅔ yard
	5901-40	⅔ yard

WOF = width of fabric

Month Two

	5901-2174	¼ yard
	8088-328	15" x WOF
	8086-328	15" x WOF

Month Three

	5901-2174	⅓ yard
	8078-335	⅜ yard
	8083-335	⅜ yard

Month Four

	5901-2174	⅜ yard
	8085-326	⅜ yard
	8084-326	⅜ yard

Month Five

	5901-2174	⅜ yard
	8089-314	15" x WOF
	8081-314	15" x WOF

Month Six

	5901-2174	1 ½ yards
	8087-328	¾ yard
	8090-314	1 yard

Month Seven

	5901-2174	1 ½ yards
	8078-333	⅝ yard
	8087-322	¾ yard
	8090-311	¾ yard

Month Eight

	5901-2174	1 yard

Month Nine

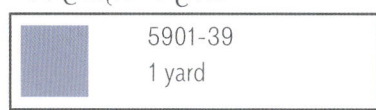

	5901-39	1 yard

Backing

	8089-328	Queen: 8 ⅓ yards
		King: 8 ⅞ yards

Month One – Hexagon Blocks

Unfinished size: 7 ½" x 7 ½"
Make five

Cutting Instructions

	Background	
	2 - 8 ½" x width of fabric strips, subcut into:	
	5 - 8 ½" squares	A
	Red Airplanes	
	1 - 7" x width of fabric strip	B
	2 - 3 ½" x width of fabric strips *(save for outer border)*	C
	Cream Scattered Flowers	
	2 - 3 ½" x width of fabric strips *(save for outer border)*	D
	1 - 3" x width of fabric strip	E

Block Instructions:

Using the Large Hexagon Template, cut five Large Hexagon Units from the Fabric B strip.

Center the Small Hexagon Template on the Large Hexagon Unit. Draw around template, then draw another line ¼" inside the first marking. Cut out the small hexagon shape on the ¼" drawn lines. This will reduce bulk and keep the darker red fabric from showing through.

Fold a Fabric A square into quarters to create center creases.

Applique a Large Hexagon Unit on a Fabric A square placing the dotted lines on creases.

Partial Hexagon Unit should measure 8 ½" x 8 ½".

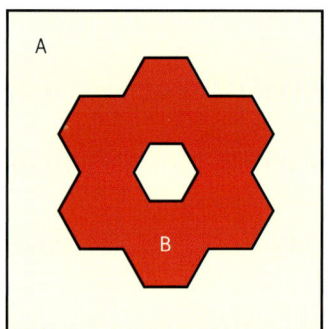

Make five.

- -

Using the Small Hexagon Template, cut five Small Hexagon Units from the Fabric E strip.

Applique a Small Hexagon Unit on a Partial Hexagon Unit.

Trim Hexagon Block to measure 7 ½" x 7 ½".

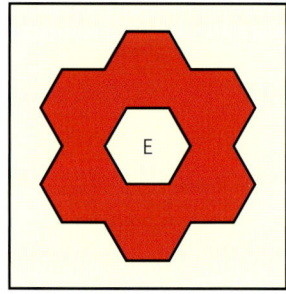

Make five.

Applique Templates and Placement Guide

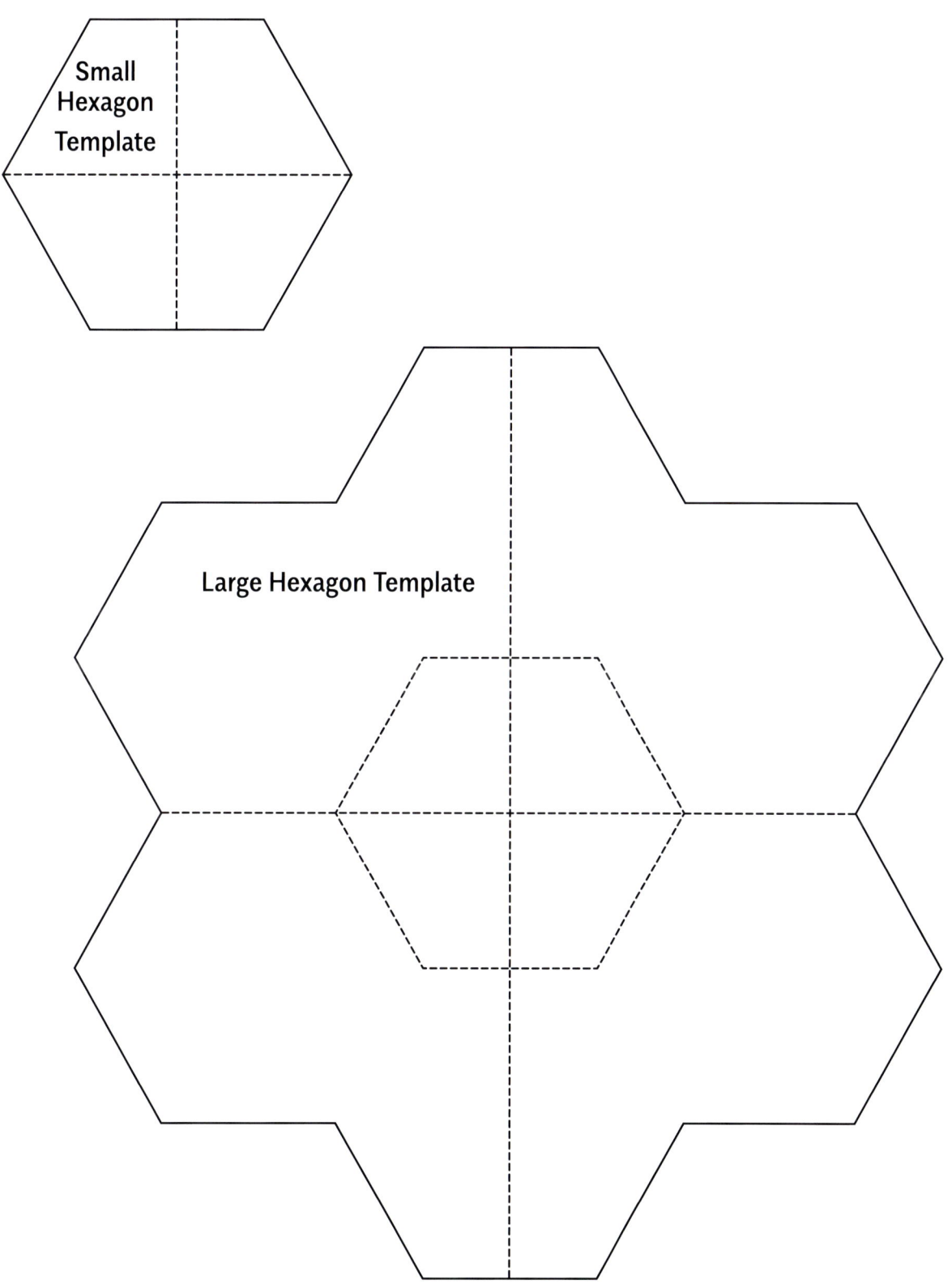

Month One – Hummingbird Blocks

Unfinished size: 6 ½" x 6 ½"
Make four total

Cutting Instructions

▨	**Background**	
	1 - 7 ½" x width of fabric strip, subcut into:	
	4 - 7 ½" squares	A
▨	**Lilac Crosses**	
	2 - 3 ½" x width of fabric strips *(save for outer border)*	B
	1 - 3" x width of fabric strip, subcut into:	
	4 - 3" squares	C
▨	**Pink Kittens**	
	2 - 3 ½" x width of fabric strips *(save for outer border)*	B
	1 - 3" x width of fabric strip, subcut into:	
	4 - 3" squares	C
▨	**Yellow Airplanes**	
	2 - 3 ½" x width of fabric strips *(save for outer border)*	D
	1 - 3" x width of fabric strip, subcut into:	
	4 - 3" squares	E
▨	**Mint Bubbles**	
	2 - 3 ½" x width of fabric strips *(save for outer border)*	D
	1 - 3" x width of fabric strip, subcut into:	
	4 - 3" squares	E

Block Instructions:

For the Hummingbird Blocks, pair a Fabric C square with a Fabric E square.

Assemble Unit.

Four Patch Unit should measure 5 ½" x 5 ½".

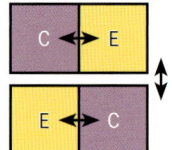  

Make two from each fabric pair. Make four total.

Using the Hummingbird Template, cut a Hummingbird Unit from a Four Patch Unit.

Applique a Hummingbird Unit on a Fabric A square.

Trim Hummingbird Block to measure 6 ½" x 6 ½".

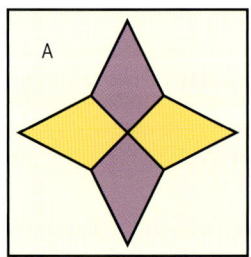 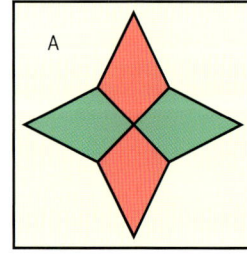

Make two from each fabric pair. Make four total.

Appliqué Template and Placement Guide

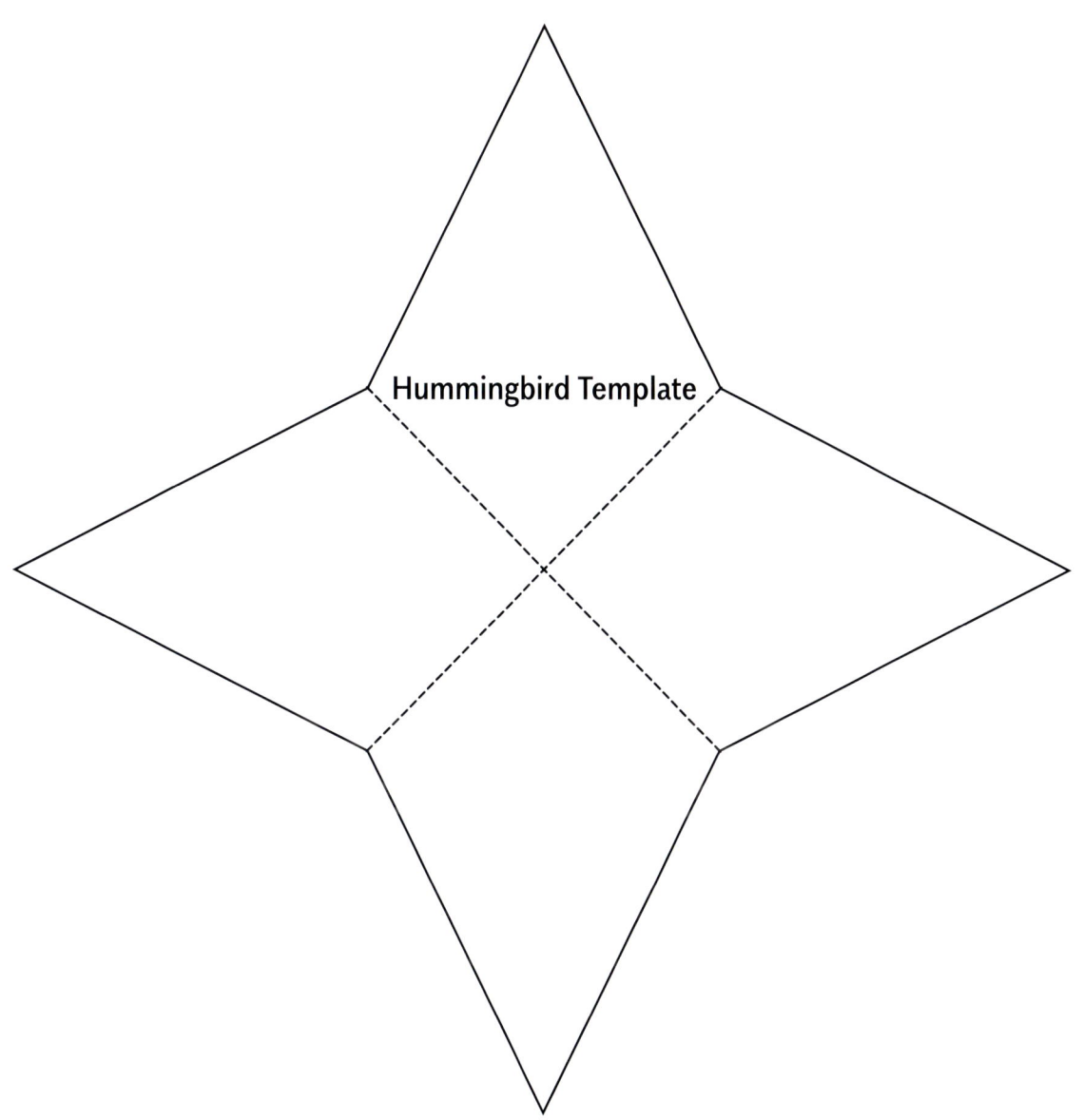

Hummingbird Template

Month One - Flourishing Leaf Blocks

Unfinished size: 9" x 9"
Make twenty

Cutting Instructions

Background
4 - 8" x width of fabric strips, subcut into:
   20 - 8" squares   A
6 - 4 ¾" x width of fabric strips, subcut into:
   20 - 4 ¾" squares   B
   40 - 2 ⅝" x 4 ¾" rectangles   C

Denim Daisies
2 - 3 ½" x width of fabric strips *(save for outer border)*   D
2 - 3" x width of fabric strips   E

Lilac Bubbles
2 - 3 ½" x width of fabric strips *(save for outer border)*   F
2 - 3" x width of fabric strips   G

Denim Ditzy Leaves
2 - 3 ½" x width of fabric strips *(save for outer border)*   H
4 - 3" x width of fabric strips   I

Pink Solid
7 - 2 ⅝" x width of fabric strips, subcut into:
   20 - 2 ⅝" x 6 ⅞" rectangles   J
   20 - 2 ⅝" x 4 ¾" rectangles   K

Block Instructions:

Assemble Strip Set.
Left Four Patch Strip Set should measure 5 ½" x 40".

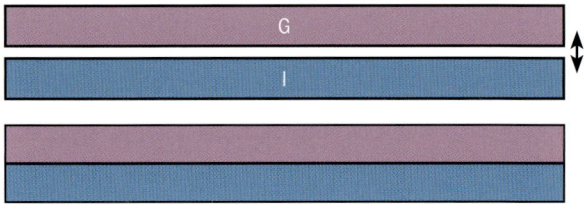

Make two.

Subcut each Left Four Patch Strip Set into ten 3" x 5 ½" rectangles.
Left Four Patch Unit should measure 3" x 5 ½".

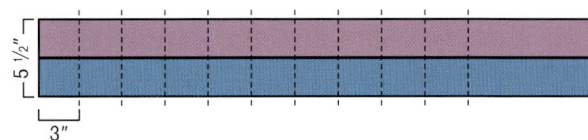

Make twenty.

Assemble Strip Set.
Right Four Patch Strip Set should measure 5 ½" x 40".

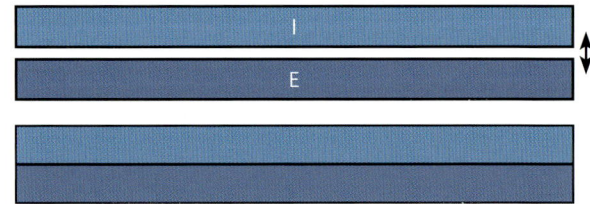

Make two.

Subcut each Right Four Patch Strip Set into ten 3" x 5 ½" rectangles.

Right Four Patch Unit should measure 3" x 5 ½".

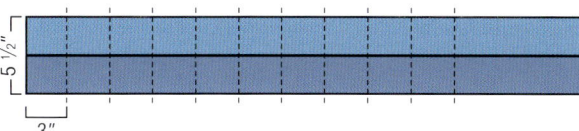

Make twenty.

Assemble Unit.

Four Patch Unit should measure 5 ½" x 5 ½".

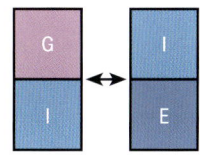 

Make twenty.

Using the Leaf Template, cut a Leaf Unit from a Four Patch Unit.

Applique a Leaf Unit on a Fabric A square.

Trim Leaf Unit to measure 6 ⅞" x 6 ⅞".

 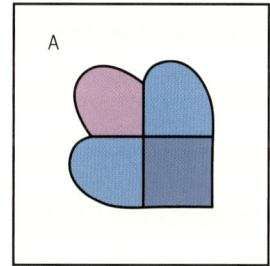

Make twenty.

On the wrong side of twenty Fabric C rectangles, mark a dot 2 ⅝" over from the top right corner. Draw a line from the bottom right corner to the dot.

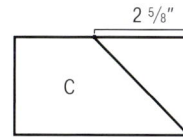

With right sides facing, layer a marked Fabric C rectangle with a Fabric J rectangle. Stitch on the drawn line and trim ¼" away from the seam.

Right Flourishing Leaf Unit should measure 2 ⅝" x 9".

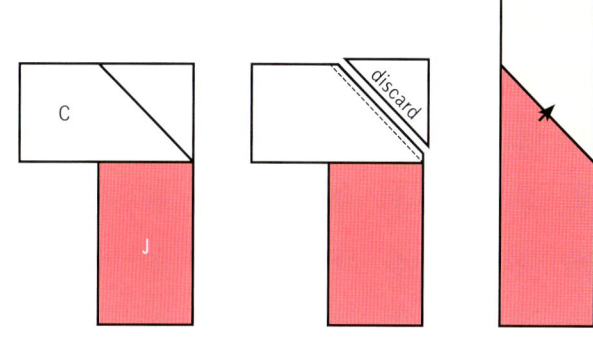

Make twenty.

Month One – Flourishing Leaf Blocks

On the wrong side of the remaining Fabric C rectangles, mark a dot 2 ⅝" up from the bottom left corner. Draw a line from the bottom right corner to the dot.

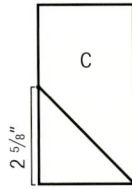

With right sides facing, layer a marked Fabric C rectangle with a Fabric K rectangle. Stitch on the drawn line and trim ¼" away from the seam.

Bottom Flourishing Leaf Unit should measure 2 ⅝" x 6 ⅞".

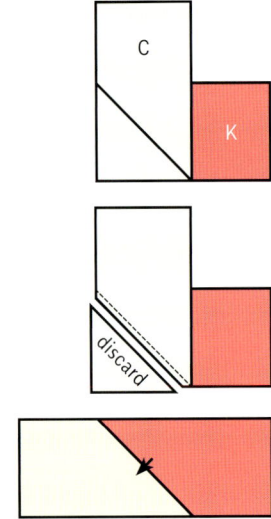

Make twenty.

Assemble Unit.

Partial Flourishing Leaf Unit should measure 9" x 9".

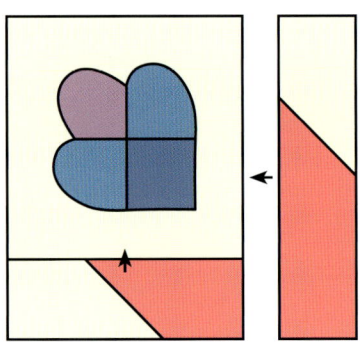

Make twenty.

Draw a diagonal line on the wrong side of the Fabric B squares.

With right sides facing, layer a Fabric B square on the bottom right corner of a Partial Flourishing Leaf Unit.

Stitch on the drawn line and trim ¼" away from the seam.

Flourishing Leaf Block should measure 9" x 9".

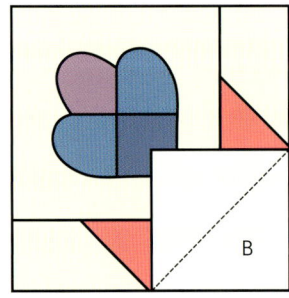 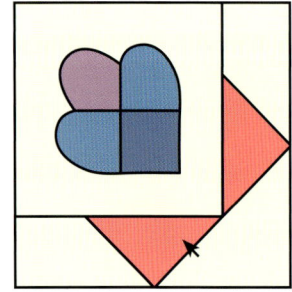

Make twenty.

Applique Template and Placement Guide

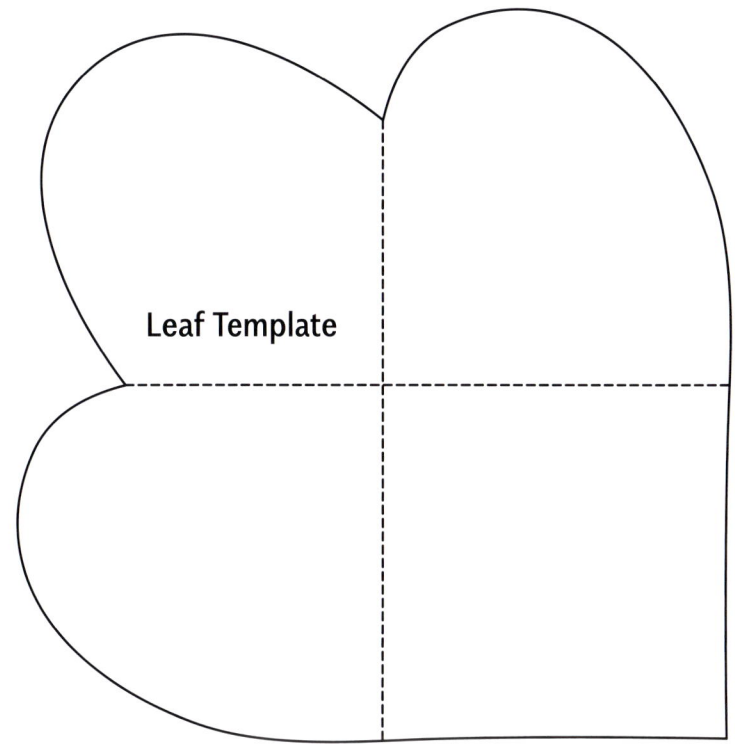

Leaf Template

Month Two - Bowties Blocks

Unfinished size: 6 ½" x 6 ½"
Make four total

Cutting Instructions

Background	
1 - 4 ¼" x width of fabric strip, subcut into:	
8 - 4 ¼" squares	A
Orange Triangles	
1 - 4 ¼" x width of fabric strip, subcut into:	
4 - 4 ¼" squares	B
2 - 3 ½" x width of fabric strips *(save for outer border)*	C
Orange Crosses	
1 - 4 ¼" x width of fabric strip, subcut into:	
4 - 4 ¼" squares	B
2 - 3 ½" x width of fabric strips *(save for outer border)*	C

Block Instructions:

Draw a diagonal line on the wrong side of the Fabric A squares.

With right sides facing, layer a Fabric A square with a Fabric B square.

Stitch ¼" from each side of the drawn line.

Cut apart on the marked line.

Half Square Triangle Unit should measure 3 ⅞" x 3 ⅞".

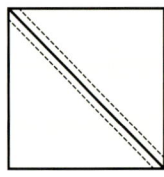 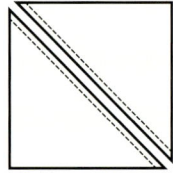 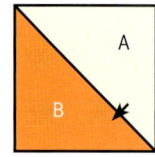

Make eight from each orange fabric. Make sixteen total.

With right sides facing, layer two matching Half Square Triangle Units.

Make sure the seams are going in the same direction.

Draw a diagonal line in the opposite direction of the seams.

Stitch ¼" from each side of the drawn line.

Cut apart on the marked line.

Quarter Square Triangle Unit should measure 3 ½" x 3 ½".

 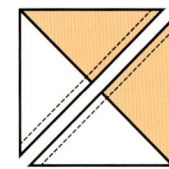 

Make eight from each orange fabric. Make sixteen total.

Assemble Block using matching fabrics.

Bowties Block should measure 6 ½" x 6 ½".

Make two from each orange fabric. Make four total.

Month Three - Garden of Eden Blocks

Unfinished size: 6 ½" x 6 ½"
Make four total

Block Instructions:

Draw a diagonal line on the wrong side of the Fabric A squares.

With right sides facing, layer a Fabric A square on one corner of a Fabric D square.

Stitch on the drawn line and trim ¼" away from the seam.

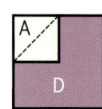 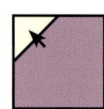

Repeat on the remaining corners.

Garden of Eden Unit should measure 3" x 3".

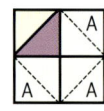 

Make eight from each lilac fabric. Make sixteen total.

Assemble Block using matching fabrics.

Garden of Eden Block should measure 6 ½" x 6 ½".

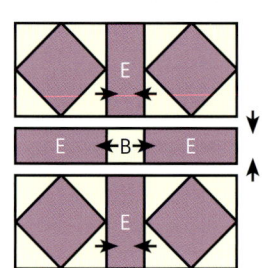 

Make two from each lilac fabric. Make four total.

Cutting Instructions

Background	
3 - 1 ¾" x width of fabric strips, subcut into:	
64 - 1 ¾" squares	A
From remainder of strip, cut:	
4 - 1 ½" squares	B
Lilac White Floral	
2 - 3 ½" x width of fabric strips *(save for outer border)*	C
1 - 3" x width of fabric strip, subcut into:	
8 - 3" squares	D
8 - 1 ½" x 3" rectangles	E
Lilac Scattered Floral	
2 - 3 ½" x width of fabric strips *(save for outer border)*	C
1 - 3" x width of fabric strip, subcut into:	
8 - 3" squares	D
8 - 1 ½" x 3" rectangles	E

Month Four - Puzzle Star Blocks

Unfinished size: 6 ½" x 6 ½"
Make four total

Block Instructions:

Draw a diagonal line on the wrong side of the Fabric A squares.

With right sides facing, layer a Fabric A square with a Fabric D square.

Stitch ¼" from each side of the drawn line.

Cut apart on the marked line.

Half Square Triangle Unit should measure 2" x 2".

 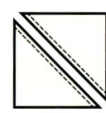

Make eight from each pink fabric. Make sixteen total.

Draw a diagonal line on the wrong side of thirty-two Fabric B squares.

With right sides facing, layer a marked Fabric B square on the top end of a Fabric E rectangle.

Stitch on the drawn line and trim ¼" away from the seam.

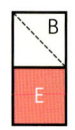 

Repeat on the bottom end.

Partial Puzzle Star Unit should measure 2" x 3 ½".

Make eight from each pink fabric. Make sixteen total.

Cutting Instructions

Background
1 - 2 ⅜" x width of fabric strip, subcut into:
    8 - 2 ⅜" squares   A

3 - 2" x width of fabric strips, subcut into:
    48 - 2" squares   B

Pink Ditzy Flowers
2 - 3 ½" x width of fabric strips *(save for outer border)*   C

1 - 2 ⅜" x width of fabric strip, subcut into:
    4 - 2 ⅜" squares   D
    From remainder of strip, cut:
    8 - 2" x 3 ½" rectangles   E

Pink Daisies
2 - 3 ½" x width of fabric strips *(save for outer border)*   C

1 - 2 ⅜" x width of fabric strip, subcut into:
    4 - 2 ⅜" squares   D
    From remainder of strip, cut:
    8 - 2" x 3 ½" rectangles   E

Assemble Unit using matching fabrics.

Puzzle Star Unit should measure 3 ½" x 3 ½".

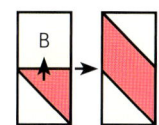 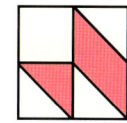

Make eight from each pink fabric. Make sixteen total.

Assemble Block using matching fabrics.

Puzzle Star Block should measure 6 ½" x 6 ½".

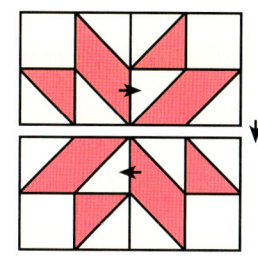 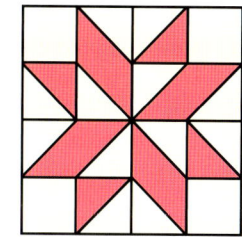

Make two from each pink fabric. Make four total.

Month Five - Mosaic Blocks

Unfinished size: 6 ½" x 6 ½"
Make four total

Block Instructions:

Draw a diagonal line on the wrong side of the Fabric A squares.

With right sides facing, layer a Fabric A square with a Fabric F square.

Stitch ¼" from each side of the drawn line.

Cut apart on the marked line.

Half Square Triangle Unit should measure 2" x 2".

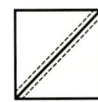 

Make eight from each green fabric. Make sixteen total.

Draw a diagonal line on the wrong side of the Fabric B squares.

With right sides facing, layer a Fabric B square on the top end of a Fabric E rectangle.

Stitch on the drawn line and trim ¼" away from the seam.

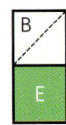 

Repeat on the bottom end.

Flying Geese Unit should measure 2" x 3 ½".

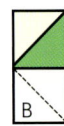 

Make eight from each green fabric. Make sixteen total.

Cutting Instructions

Background
1 - 2 ⅜" x width of fabric strip, subcut into:
    8 - 2 ⅜" squares — A
3 - 2" x width of fabric strips, subcut into:
    48 - 2" squares — B

Green Children
2 - 3 ½" x width of fabric strips *(save for outer border)* — C
1 - 3 ½" x width of fabric strip, subcut into:
    2 - 3 ½" squares — D
    8 - 2" x 3 ½" rectangles — E
From remainder of strip, cut:
    4 - 2 ⅜" squares — F

Green Patchwork
2 - 3 ½" x width of fabric strips *(save for outer border)* — C
1 - 3 ½" x width of fabric strip, subcut into:
    2 - 3 ½" squares — D
    8 - 2" x 3 ½" rectangles — E
From remainder of strip, cut:
    4 - 2 ⅜" squares — F

With right sides facing, layer a Fabric B square on one corner of a Fabric D square.

Stitch on the drawn line and trim ¼" away from the seam.

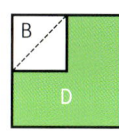 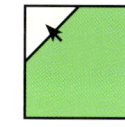

Repeat on the remaining corners.

Center Unit should measure 3 ½" x 3 ½".

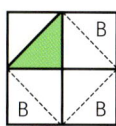 

Make two from each green fabric. Make four total.

Assemble Block using matching fabrics.

Mosaic Block should measure 6 ½" x 6 ½".

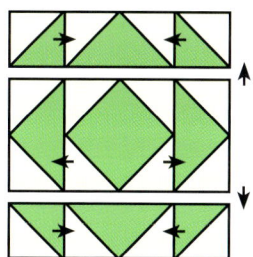 

Make two from each green fabric. Make four total.

Month Six - Big Block One

Unfinished size: 24 ½" x 24 ½"
Make five

Cutting Instructions

	Background	
	3 - 8 ¼" x width of fabric strips, subcut into:	
	10 - 8 ¼" squares	A
	5 - 4 ¾" x width of fabric strips, subcut into:	
	20 - 4 ¾" x 7 ½" rectangles	B
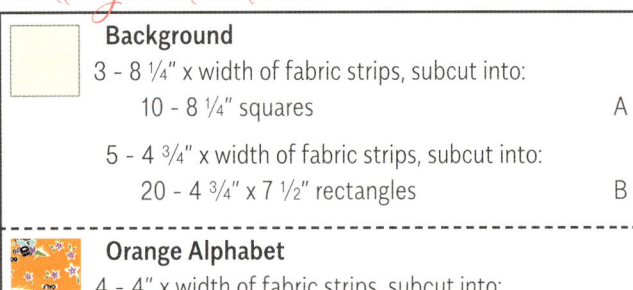	**Orange Alphabet**	
	4 - 4" x width of fabric strips, subcut into:	
	40 - 4" squares	C
	2 - 3 ½" x width of fabric strips *(save for outer border)*	D
	Mint Kittens	
	3 - 8 ¼" x width of fabric strips, subcut into:	
	10 - 8 ¼" squares	E
	2 - 3 ½" x width of fabric strips *(save for outer border)*	F

Block Instructions:

Draw a diagonal line on the wrong side of the Fabric C squares.

With right sides facing, layer a Fabric C square on the bottom left corner of a Fabric B rectangle.

Stitch on the drawn line and trim ¼" away from the seam.

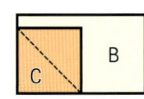 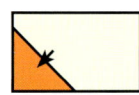

Repeat on the bottom right corner.

Top Big Block One Unit should measure 4 ¾" x 7 ½".

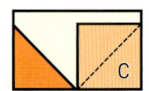 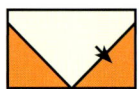

Make twenty.

Draw a diagonal line on the wrong side of the Fabric A squares.

With right sides facing, layer a Fabric A square with a Fabric E square.

Stitch ¼" from each side of the drawn line.

Cut apart on the marked line.

Half Square Triangle Unit should measure 7 ⅞" x 7 ⅞".

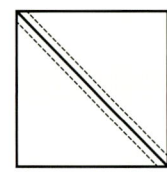 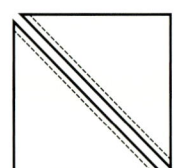 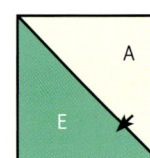

Make twenty.

With right sides facing, layer two Half Square Triangle Units.
Make sure the seams are going in the same direction.
Draw a diagonal line in the opposite direction of the seams.
Stitch ¼" from each side of the drawn line.
Cut apart on the marked line.
Quarter Square Triangle Unit should measure 7 ½" x 7 ½".

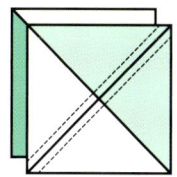 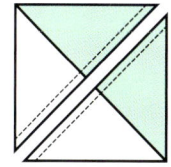 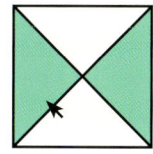

Make twenty.

Trim Bottom Big Block One Unit to measure 4 ¾" x 7 ½".

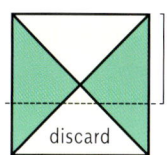  

Make twenty.

Assemble Unit.
Big Block One Unit should measure 7 ½" x 9".

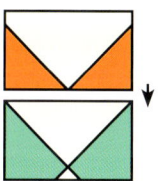 

Make twenty.

Assemble Block using four Big Block One Units, four Flourishing Leaf Blocks from Month One and one Hexagon Block from Month One.

Big Block One should measure 24 ½" x 24 ½".

Make five.

Month Seven - Big Block Two

Unfinished size: 24 ½" x 24 ½"
Make two

Unfinished size: 24 ½" x 24 ½"
Make two

Cutting Instructions

Background		
10 - 3 ½" x width of fabric strips, subcut into:		
48 - 3 ½" x 6 ½" rectangles		A
16 - 3 ½" squares		B
2 - 4 ½" x width of fabric strips		C
2 - 2 ½" x width of fabric strips		D
Yellow White Floral		
2 - 3 ½" x width of fabric strips *(save for outer border)*		E
3 - 2 ½" x width of fabric strips		F
Blue Alphabet		
2 - 3 ½" x width of fabric strips *(save for outer border)*		G
4 - 3 ½" x width of fabric strips, subcut into:		
32 - 3 ½" squares		H
Red Kittens		
2 - 3 ½" x width of fabric strips *(save for outer border)*		I
4 - 3 ½" x width of fabric strips, subcut into:		
32 - 3 ½" squares		J

Block Instructions:

Assemble Strip Set.

Outside Partial Corner Strip Set should measure 6 ½" x 40".

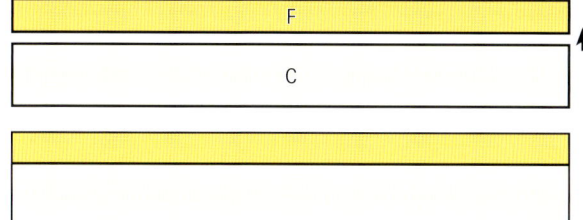

Make two.

Subcut each Outside Partial Corner Strip Set into sixteen 2 ½" x 6 ½" rectangles.

Outside Partial Corner Unit should measure 2 ½" x 6 ½".

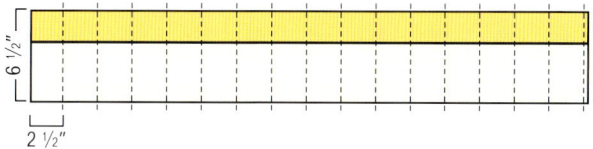

Make thirty-two.

Assemble Strip Set.

Inside Partial Corner Strip Set should measure 6 ½" x 40".

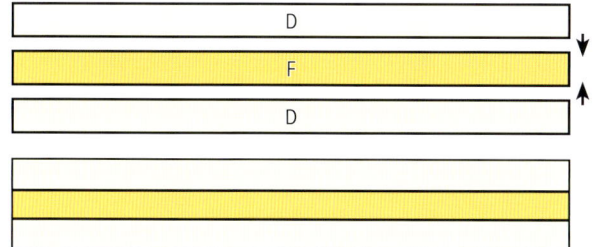

Make one.

Subcut the Inside Partial Corner Strip Set into sixteen 2 ½" x 6 ½" rectangles.

Inside Partial Corner Unit should measure 2 ½" x 6 ½".

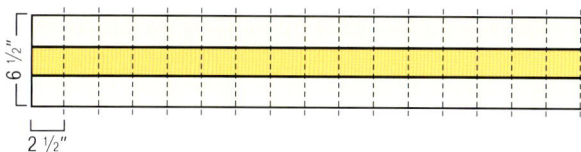

Make sixteen.

Assemble Unit.

Partial Corner Unit should measure 6 ½" x 6 ½".

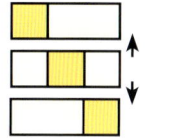

Make sixteen.

Draw a diagonal line on the wrong side of the Fabric H squares.

With right sides facing, layer a Fabric H square on the bottom end of a Fabric A rectangle.

Stitch on the drawn line and trim ¼" away from the seam.

Right Corner Unit should measure 3 ½" x 6 ½".

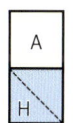

Make sixteen.

With right sides facing, layer a Fabric H square on the right end of a Fabric A rectangle.

Stitch on the drawn line and trim ¼" away from the seam.

Bottom Corner Unit should measure 3 ½" x 6 ½".

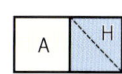 

Make sixteen.

Month Seven - Big Block Two

Assemble Unit.

Corner Unit should measure 9 ½" x 9 ½".

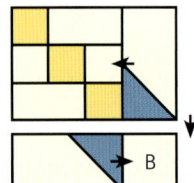 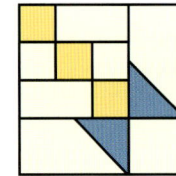

Make sixteen.

Draw a diagonal line on the wrong side of the Fabric J squares.

With right sides facing, layer a Fabric J square on one end of a Fabric A rectangle.

Stitch on the drawn line and trim ¼" away from the seam.

Repeat on the opposite end.

Flying Geese Unit should measure 3 ½" x 6 ½".

Make sixteen.

Assemble Unit using a Bowties Block from Month Two.

Top Big Block Two Unit should measure 6 ½" x 9 ½".

Make four.

Assemble Unit using a Mosaic Block from Month Five.

Left Big Block Two Unit should measure 6 ½" x 9 ½".

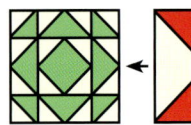 

Make four.

Assemble Unit using a Garden of Eden Block from Month Three.

Right Big Block Two Unit should measure 6 ½" x 9 ½".

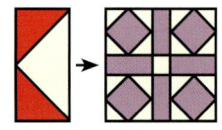 

Make four.

Assemble Unit using a Puzzle Star Block from Month Four.

Bottom Big Block Two Unit should measure 6 ½" x 9 ½".

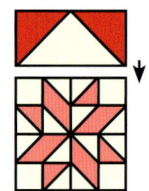 

Make four.

Assemble Block using Four Corner Units, one Top Big Block Two Unit, one Left Big Block Two Unit, one Hummingbird Block from Month One, one Right Big Block Two Unit and one Bottom Big Block Two Unit.

Top/Bottom Big Block Two should measure 24 ½" x 24 ½".

Make two identical blocks using coordinating fabrics.

Assemble Block using Four Corner Units, one Right Big Block Two Unit, one Top Big Block Two Unit, one Hummingbird Block from Month One, one Bottom Big Block Two Unit and one Left Big Block Two Unit.

Sides Big Block Two should measure 24 ½" x 24 ½".

Make two identical blocks using coordinating fabrics.

Month Eight - Quilt Center & Inner Border

Cutting Instructions

Background
9 - 3 ½" x width of fabric strips, sew end to end and subcut into:
- 2 - 3 ½" x 78 ½" strips — A
- 2 - 3 ½" x 72 ½" strips — B

Quilt Center Assembly:

Assemble Quilt Center. Press rows in opposite directions.
Quilt Center should measure 72 ½" x 72 ½".

Month Eight - Quilt Center & Inner Border

Inner Border:

Attach side inner borders using the Fabric B strips.

Attach top and bottom inner borders using the Fabric A strips.

Month Nine - Queen Outer Border & Finishing

90 ½" x 96 ½"

Queen Cutting Instructions

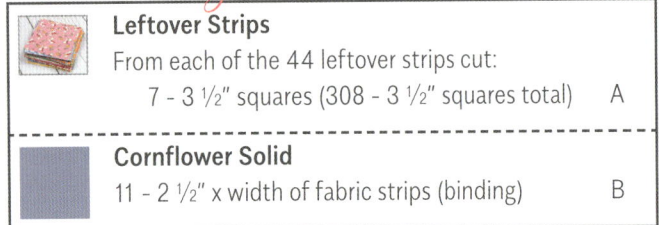

	Leftover Strips	
	From each of the 44 leftover strips cut: 7 - 3 ½" squares (308 - 3 ½" squares total)	A
	Cornflower Solid	
	11 - 2 ½" x width of fabric strips (binding)	B

Queen Outer Border:

Assemble two rows of twenty-six Fabric A squares *(one hundred four Fabric A squares total)*.

Side Outer Border should measure 6 ½" x 78 ½".

Make two.

Assemble three rows of thirty Fabric A squares *(one hundred eighty Fabric A squares total)*.

You will not use all Fabric A squares.

Top and Bottom Outer Border should measure 9 ½" x 90 ½".

Make two.

Attach the Side Outer Borders.

Attach the Top and Bottom Outer Borders.

Queen Finishing

Piece the Fabric B strips end to end for binding.

Quilt and bind as desired.

Month Nine – King Outer Border & Finishing

96 ½" x 102 ½"

King Cutting Instructions

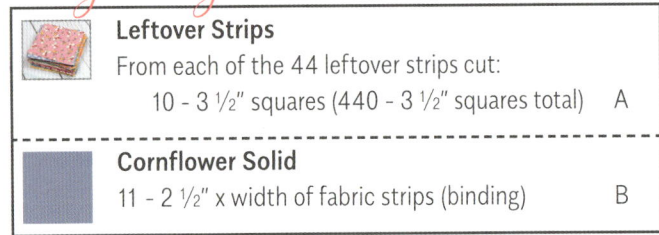

Leftover Strips
From each of the 44 leftover strips cut:
10 - 3 ½" squares (440 - 3 ½" squares total)   A

Cornflower Solid
11 - 2 ½" x width of fabric strips (binding)   B

King Outer Border:

Assemble three rows of twenty-six Fabric A squares *(one hundred fifty-six Fabric A squares total)*.

Side Outer Border should measure 9 ½" x 78 ½".

Make two.

Assemble four rows of thirty-two Fabric A squares *(two hundred fifty-six Fabric A squares total)*.

You will not use all Fabric A squares.

Top and Bottom Outer Border should measure 12 ½" x 96 ½".

Make two.